CIRCULARITIES

by

Robert Myers

NORTHWEST
PASSAGE
Books

Circularities

by Bob Myers

ISBN: 978-1-9991146-3-3

Published by
Northwest Passage Books
Gatineau, Quebec, Canada

Front cover design by Linda Myers

Other poetry titles by Myers:

An Economy of Words
(Northwest Passage Books, 2018)

CONTENTS

For my wife Linda.
fifty years of loving
and praying together.

CIRCULARITIES

TAKING POSSESSION

The door opens inward. Echo chamber.
Footfall and first words fill the hollow,
round out corners and creases.
The house takes a breath of fresh air,
mingles with yours like spun gold.
The baby squirms in your arms and reaches.
This is your home. Was always your home.
A future already remembered.

PRESENTIMENT

Summer heat fell and preyed
on the village pitilessly. Thickened air
everywhere. Visible fever heat swayed
skyward from ailing houses. Water glare
shimmered on black empty streets.
Leaves in their prime and flowers
defeated by heat, surrendered at last
like lifeless limbs and failure.
Nowhere nor at any hour
did birdsong gladden men's hearts.
Only the Mourning Dove's drowsier
shallow appeal. Grave. Uninspired.

Another dread more suppressive
than Summer heat preyed on mankind,
a far-reaching menace ill-advised
to ignore. Across the heavens trumpets blared.
Heavenly seals broke wide open and flared.
New-fashioned signal fire warnings
before the enemy comes. O Mercy Divine!
Discomfort our swoon! Open our heavy eyes!

3

LIGHT LINES

My grandmother heard it before
anyone else, the baritone rumble-roll
torment of thunder. "Dangerous.
From the East," she said, wringing
her hands on her apron, closing the door.
"Jesus, Mary and Joseph! Open all
the windows. Quick now. God help us!"
Another deep grumble, this one lingering
for all to hear. Then a whitewash
invasion of light sweeping the house clear.
"Open the windows." (Signing the cross.)
"If a ball comes in it has to go out the same.
We'll say the Rosary against them who'd harm us."
We thought her a superstitious old dear
believing lightning could enter a house,
that somehow the fairies were to blame,
their punishment for someone who'd foolishly
trod on their path or didn't believe.

I turned on the TV last night, tuned in
the weather report on high definition, live-
streaming satellite imagery, doppler
radar, fifty-five inch screen technology.
The meteorologist swept in, her tiger skin
mini all swivel and curve.
She waved her long arm over isobars.
"A severe thunderstorm warning for all
these regions…" and on she droned.
Then her expression turned thoughtful.
"Scientists are trying to understand
the phenomenon known as lightning balls."
(We see images of two gaping holes
in a wide-bodied Aer Lingus jet full
of passengers that had tried to land
in a storm.) "With such damage, it's a miracle
no one was hurt, a frequent flyer told us."

I checked the internet. Saw another interview
with the cautious pilot, a modern Galway man
with no explanation to give.
(His manner professionally curt.)
I am a modern man too,
but pressed I think I'd side with my gran.
I know what I believe.
What flyers and science cannot.

THE CALL

Driving. Kawartha Lakes.
September preparing her palate
in earnest now. Her canvas
the sky and trees.
Today, out of control
temper and brushes;
She cannot find a vanishing point.

Overhead, great grey clouds
close enough to touch,
roll and roil and dump
their loads over the whole world.
The sky is falling
but we dare not stop.
We drive beside forests
we cannot see.
The wipers can't keep up.
Headlights are futile.
We are driving drowned.

She curses the dismal
half-light, ready to pack it in,
another Autumn day swallowed
by seasonal intemperance.
She cannot find a starting point.

Then, around a sweeping bend,
a slanting Caravaggion beam
of light slices across,
right to left.
A ray of hope calling us home.
We are released.

She seizes the chance
and a quick deft brush.
Poplar trees appear.
She helps them remember
their yellow-green Spring leaves
before painting them gold
with age.

The light persists.
Spirits lift.
On the radio
Gershwin's Lullaby
for String Quartet.

CIRCULARITIES

I

As children when we held the nub
of a stick to drive the wood hoop
through an invisible route ahead,
it rolled onward in present tenses,
the behind our heels gone forever.
To keep the hoop controlled alongside
our unhurried happiness, we gauged
each stroke with practiced wisdom
known only to children. Otherwise
it purchased momentum and flew
unbalanced, bouncing, careening,
leaning, dancing over every pebble
and crack out of alignment with itself
and time. Until time wore it down.

Energy spent, it flipped over,
a spasmodic circle of clattering,
hurrying itself silent and still.

Staring ahead over the steering wheel's
curve I thought about hoops today;
their unmelodiousness, their perpetual
roundedness, listening and looking
back to a memory. No, more than a memory.
An inviolate souvenir, perhaps.

ll

But not even perhaps.
Clutching my hand for assurance
a grandson hops to school
upon black asphalt sealant
ribbons, irregular orbits all over
everywhere into the cul-de-sac.
Here begins the impenetrable forest.
Dark as fear. No going back.
Inside, yesterday's path is gone,
overgrown or concealed. This way
and that we press on, step on
a fairy ring and are lost. He knows
the curse. Finds his pluck. Pulls
my weighted pretence onward. Through.

lll

His mother loved Granuaile
or at least the romance of piracy
by which she thrived. At Rockfleet
she took the lead traipsing up
the winding stone stairway set
like a gyre inside square walls,
winding upwards into the past.
Slightly giddy upon arrival
she nevertheless circled the great
room three times then sat
by the fireplace, half her face
hidden by shadow and cascading hair.
I can still see that now. That aery tableau.
Her flared apparition. Her Grace.

IV

After Mass the Sunday morning fry-up;
bacon, sausages, eggs, mushrooms,
tomatoes, onions, tea and soda bread. Toasted.
You loved to pierce selected bits
together for maximum flavour you said.
Pork saltiness, onion sweetness, tomato
acidity, all at peace on your tongue.
A wash of tea then a new fusion.
Toast had a different destiny.
It carried lashings of jam you made
last year, saved 'till the plate was clear.
Then tea dredges, black and not hot.
After Mass Sunday mornings,
our ritual Irishry, sacred as a pledge.

V

You never put too much stock
in owning things. All you ever asked
was fundamental; food, shelter, clothing
and thank God for these. The rest
money can't buy; love, family, friends.
Once you pondered, even marvelled at
ancient information technology painted
on cave walls. Food, shelter, clothing
and a hand, confident and assertive,
"I was here." So leave your own mark.
Emblazon with love those you love,
family and friends. Leave your mark upon
their eternal souls, assertive and indelible.
Your legacy after everything else decays.

VI

Round gone flat
like a Plane Trajectory.
Your forty square foot black canvas
looked more a sky map; white paint
dots for stars, planets, galaxies, distorted
fragments, curvatures, puzzle perfect
already deciphered in your mind's eye.
Your own Book of Kells—Bayeux Tapestry
hybrid, knot-worked, birded, tail-eating
serpented, marvellously understood.
When all connects, the woven braids
translate under your wizard touch.
Your concept realised comes full
circle from fantasy to form.

VII

Standing water stink.
Bog water reek.
You drove the plunger vigorously
into the drain, vigorously withdrew,
the squelch and slurp
like wellingtons siphoning, pumping
bog water out of, back into itself
one step at a time. For an hour
you plunged deeper into the depths
of your own obstinate will until
that sweet singing whirlpool
sucked everything away, leaving
triumphant emptiness.
But nothing insignificant.

VIII

He loves to tell about the week
he manoeuvred Mosquitos around
the aerodrome, into the hanger
without touching the plane. Bent
like a longbow, calves string taut,
puffing noisily while others obediently
pushed, his hands shadowing the fraud.
A young warrior's wily dodge
unweighting war's weariness.
A hundred years have failed
to diminish his mischievous misconducts.
Throttle finesse, subtle manoeuvrability,
his wheelchair dodging tables, chairs, staff.
The ancient warrior's canny joie de vivre.

IX

Locked down. Confined to room.
Soft knocking on the door at 5 p.m.
Their meal, meagre, institutional,
delivered, this day's only interruption
to wearisome timelessness,
the wages a virus exacts.
He might be thinking how they came
to this. He asks her to sift through
her memory backwards seventy years
to that bliss-filled wedding day,
whose sacred vows meant something
then, not now, whose days were
never ever left unspent,
whose quiet harmonies still sail along.

X

When we entered Schneider's Woods,
how many times now, eight? ten?
we burdened ourselves with doubts.
The main loop, painted trees
easy to follow, an hour tops,
well trafficked, returned us here
where we now stand, deciding.
In there, off-branches less travelled
cross lesser worn options
and, where few feet have trod,
our present fears await.
So let's trespass on fear, discharge doubts,
trample thicket and thorn at least
once before we head for home.

XI

The village's central compactness,
a crossroad mill whereabouts, lends
itself to walking tours or more invitingly
in the French manner, *promenades*
leisurely taken. All ways eventually
enfold the pond's placid presence.
You love the terse tension of grey
black-necked geese watching from
water's edge or crowding your footpath
ahead. Daring you. How the clipped confident
approaching horses, their buggy's lyrical
creakings hearten your outing.
How your presence ever so gently
impresses upon the scene.

Xll

Sometime ago in an age
less commerced and lost
the mill drew a daily influx
of tackle and trade and talk.
Its timbers nowadays house
antiques and muted nostalgia.
Tourists take photographs hoping
to encounter their own pipe-dreams.
You knew the hew and haul
of mills, the steadfast water race,
the less hurried scramble.
You knew that some time ago,
but at the same time not at the time
how elusive it would become.

XIII

Elusive as molten mercury,
tangible yet untouchable
or like vintage wines cellared
in the depths of your mind waiting
to be released, so memories lie
and will die lest given life
in others' morrow years.
Some sudden scrap of phrase,
a sound, a whiff, a photograph
and you are turned around;
a schoolyard crush, the pain of loss,
a secret fear. Do not withhold.
Do not withhold, do not.
The aftermath's too dear.

XIV

St. Augustine said before
we explore the wondrous world
we should wonder at ourselves.
We were made at the start
as he well knew, in God's own image
and likeness, a portrait of our creator.
After the third day He entered
their chamber and said, "Do you have
anything to eat?" Again beside the lake,
"Cook some fish for me." Alive. Glorified.
Transcendent flesh and blood,
and yes, corporeal Garden of Eden
God and man. The saint posing
a prelude of past perfection to come.

XV

Whatever they knew, they knew
as certainty; good money
could be made in the catching
and selling of fish. The outlay—
a boat, a net, strong backs,
knowledge of winds, seasons,
the how and where of fish in their numbers.
These reliabilities they knew. Trusted.
"Follow me and I will make you
fishers of men."
Didn't anyone ask why?
Is there money involved? Where
are we going? Their fathers in the boats
still shouting. Their nets still un-hauled.

XVI

When He was out walking He noticed
a tax collector and said to him,
"Follow me." And leaving everything
he got up and followed Him.
And to others, *"Follow me."*
Certainties abandoned, thrown
upon two words from
a passing carpenter's son.
Theirs was not the fear of God,
nor doubt nor awe, not these
but a matter-of-fact acceptance
of authority, of providence.
As easy as walking on water.
As easy as forgiving sin.

XVII

Hours it took and tedious, the circular
business of passing a camel
through the eye of the needle.
Unloading the beast, then through
the narrow back door, reloading
on the other side like a fresh start,
the penultimate stage along
a long and difficult road.
What must I do? He asked.
"Sell what you have, give the money
to the poor and follow me."
But he was heavy of heart,
standing at the threshold
loathe to unload.

XVIII

By pulling the bedcovers over
our heads we entered a secret
moment between father and son
and an unexpected birthday surprise.
He fired the cap gun four
or five times, the sparks
shorting the darkness like lightning
from his hand, the faint smell
of cordite unable to escape
fuelling my panic and fear.
I heard him call I should be proud
of my military heritage
as I ran from the room
leaving the past in its shrouded tomb.

XIX

If you stood behind the howitzer
you could watch the shot projectile
arc across the sky before it disappeared
and fell unseen on its target
blowing to bits materials and men.
A tug of the lanyard.
Death by remote control.
You didn't think of this as you fired
round after round after round
on its far away mission,
only the beauty of the arc
repeating across the glorious sky.
Every twenty seconds another arc.
Precise geometry clean and exact.

XX

Long ago I dreamed my father came
over a hill on crutches wide apart
of his one-and-a-half legs. A war hero
coming home. I ran to meet him
wanting to jump into his arms.
His own father had commanded a horse regiment
in the "war to end all wars," but instead
of coming home, had abandoned him.
I have photographs of both warriors
dressed out like *'hommes fatals.'*
My grandfather was a bigamist, his son
an adulterer. I dreamt a lie.
Not all casualties of war are dead.
Not all casualties of war shed blood.

LIKE SMALL WHITE MOTHS

Like small white moths lost,
little snowflakes flit
soundlessly, free falling,
spiralling, alighting finally
among their frail fellows below.

Like small white moths a host
has come from who-knows-
where without notice,
until they were always here
beyond these white framed windows.

Like small white moths tossed
lightly from an unknowable sky
indifferently pale, aimless and
hushed, left and right,
lift and drift, they fall and fall.

Like small white moths washed
in single minded innocence,
unaware of flight's end
in January's cold morning air,
buoyant in collective flight.

Like small white moths untouched
by sadness or joy, crystalline,
immaculate, ambulant, silent
witnesses to life short-lived
purposefully, wondrously, Godly.

A BOOK FALLEN

In another poem someone called
the day —did he mean *every* day?—
"intolerable." You said you recalled
sitting on the sofa in the bay

window reading these astonishing
lines while on your shoulders slanting beams
of sunlight set the dusty air dancing
like a prelude to a drowsy dream.

That was a February day and you
lifted your head abruptly to the fire
frowning, wondering if you'd misconstrued
the text or failed to see the underlie.

Maybe he abhorred the sight of light
for reasons not revealed, imprisoning
himself behind drawn curtains mole-like,
the thumb of his last candle flickering

against the darkness blackening his heart.
This image grew inside your mind and then
a piece of wood fell over with a sharp
snap and you were lucid once again.

By now the room was toasty warm and night
approaching. From the fire hot air was pouring
out in waves against the feeble light.
Right! You said. This needs investigating.

But the book was on the floor beside your feet,
Fallen from your fingers. Shut. The page,
the title, writer, everything was gone.
And you slouched and cursed and fumed like a smoking bomb.

AFTERBIRTH

B.C. In Memoriam

At the most critical moment
they were alone in that room,
mother and child, she and
her beautiful baby boy,
the fruit of her womb.

Moments before she felt
the voice of an angel touch her heart;
"Pray now for the two of you."
And the Chaplet of Mercy was told.

She wasn't prepared for this;
the cord entangled around his neck,
the light of life leaving his face,
the rest of his body inert.

She fumbles a gadget for help
fearing they'll never arrive in time
and takes the task on herself
searching a sharp edge,
cradling her son in her arms
gently, carefully, not ever
to quit her embrace,
slashing away at the cord
to save her boy

slashing her own flesh too
as she fights for his life.

Holding his weight awkwardly.
Telling him all will be right.

Then he is gone.

Someone is wrapping her injured hand.
She watches them hover over her child.
Detached now.
Her clear mind admires
their controlled urgency,
their skilled hands at work.

Sees the light of hope drain
from their eyes.

"Oh God!" She cries aloud
and the room stops.
"Oh God! How will I tell his wife and kids?"

FEAR

Fear is a lethal immobilizer invading the body like a slow moving fire-worm liquifying the brain to useless mush while limbs slump torpid and inert. Rational thought abandons the mind, the mouth becomes dry as sand, vision blurs, breathing shallows unable to deliver enough oxygen to a hammering heart. Nothing can be done. Nothing can be done as the tunnel of darkness closes in swallowing everything known into a valley of death.

Fear is a powerful stimulant smashing home like a mule kick, mobilising mind and body, igniting action learned or spontaneous, turning boys into men and men into boys. Fear sharpens the wits as the sudden injection of adrenalin fires body and mind to decide something must be done.

Fear visited Joe and Paddy at the dawning of a day in May 1943 'though neither one was aware of the other's existence. Paddy was on his second tour of duty as a tail gunner in a Lancaster heavy bomber commonly called the "Lanc." They were returning to England from a bombing raid over Hamburg where submarine pens and industries of war had been hammered for the past few weeks. As a twenty-three year-old volunteer from neutral Ireland he had the respect and affection of the other seven crew members especially as the tail gunner was often the first casualty of Luftwaffe fighter attacks. On every mission fear rode along comfortably in his gut almost to the point of indifference. He had compartmentalized each flight into Six Stages starting with the slow bomb laden crossing of the North

Sea, the entry into Nazi occupied Europe and anti-aircraft flak fields, the nerve wracking level bomb run over the target, the turn for home into swarms of fighters and interceptors, surviving these attacks to the North Sea and finally, hopefully, arriving home in one piece. As he ticked each box in the eight hour journey, fear became a manageable commodity which he could acknowledge but never take for granted. Bomber Command had the highest loss rate among Allied aircraft in the Second World War and on many missions, dozens of his friends never returned. For Paddy the war provided a diversion from idleness and when in RAF dress attire, his boyish good looks, dark wavy hair, charming smile and Irish brogue reduced many a lovely English girl to eager willingness. During these encounters Paddy knew no fear.

Eleven-year-old Joe had aged dramatically since his eighth birthday, March 11, 1940. For one thing, words that didn't exist before were now part of his everyday conversation and behaviour since the German Army rolled into and took control of Haarlem, the Dutch town he called home. The new vocabulary had many different meanings but the common thread among them was the fear they disseminated. Joe's world was one of regular interrogations, the Gestapo, The SS para-military brigades, Nazi SD intelligence men, NSB (the hated Dutch collaborators) and the terrifying Razzia! The Razzia arrived in trucks at a town centre or small village when all the men aged 18-40 were rounded up for slave labour duties. Anyone caught hiding a man from the Razzia could be shot. In three years Joe's childhood games had evolved into adult games, hiding downed Allied airmen, delivering secret "Underground" messages, sabotaging construction sites and stealing German weapons. He had learned how to make himself invisible to the occupiers by being obvious whether he was helping his father deliver milk or playing marbles with his pals. His fear was tempered by his few years and the innocent conviction that nothing bad was ever going to happen to him.

This morning as Paddy's Lanc approached his Stage Four, the pilot braced the crew for a change of course over the Netherlands instead of the North Sea, a more dangerous route calculated to reduce their flying time by nearly an hour. Now six hours into their mission they had become stragglers escorting a "lame duck" Lanc limping home on two Merlins, the port engines seriously damaged by flak. They were shadowing the wounded Lanc about 50 metres behind and below to provide some protection from attacks by enemy aircraft. At 6,000 ft. both crews were praying for a miracle and sleepy German defences. Paddy's parachute hung on a hook behind his gun turret useless if they had to bail out in a hurry. The turret's perspex facing was removed to offer unobstructed sight lines but his electrically heated flight suit barely kept him from shivering to death. He was tired but alert as he spotted the two fighters closing in on them, one directly behind, the other slightly below their flight path. Suddenly he experienced something he thought he had conquered over the past several months. The knot in his stomach tightened and his bowels were becoming very uncomfortable. When he recognised a deadly pair of Junkers 88 heavily armed fighters and prepared his own machine guns, he realised there was a good chance he might not survive this attack.

Having finished his morning chores Joe was following his brother Jerry along the dyke behind his house looking for some mischief. They were clambering about an old wagon when he heard the sound of aircraft approaching from the East. He looked up and saw two big airplanes, one of them trailing black smoke, being pursued by two smaller ones, all of them on a downward trajectory toward his town. He pointed them out to Jerry and they decided to take in the show like kids watching a movie. The planes were a few kilometres away yet but he reckoned they would soon pass over his neighbourhood. He became a little nervous when his sharp eyes told him the smoking plane was losing altitude faster and might not clear the houses. His father was working but his mother was at home, too far away for Joe to reach in time.

This was a different kind of fear for Joe. Here was death falling from the sky towards his own home and if it didn't hit that, he and Jerry would certainly be crushed when the plane crash landed on the dyke. Their adventure movie was about to become too real and people were going to die. The boys were momentarily paralysed by fear, stuck to the wagon boards, each waiting for the other to decide or for an intervention from God knows where.

As the Junkers closed in for the kill, Paddy knew he must focus upon one hoping the other tail gunner would take the second. Enemy fighter pilots long knew the Lancaster had no lower gun turrets and a favourite tactic was to attack from below climbing at the bomber, guns blazing away. He was shocked and surprised then when he saw one of them bank slightly down to his right then start a climb towards the other bomber. Both were going after the damaged plane first before attacking his. Paddy thought the pilot must be crazy! By this manoeuvre he would have to pass directly across his firing line giving him a few precious seconds to do some damage. He giggled with childish delight. It was an answer to a prayer too good to be true. He took a deep breath to control his excitement and waited. He heard the other fighter's bullets slam into the damaged Lanc and from the corner of his eye saw a second trail of smoke. Then his fighter filled his gun sights and he fired a long burst into the bulbous cabin housing its four crewmen. Seconds later the sky was empty. He did not see his "probable kill" veer away from the battle nor the pursuing fighter following the doomed Lanc across the Dutch roads and houses a steady stream of shells hitting and missing its target. His own pilot had throttled up passing over Haarlem and they were racing towards the coast and the relative safety of the sea. He allowed himself a smile of relief. Stage Five, here we come!

With two engines gone, another on fire and not enough altitude for bailing out, a crash landing was inevitable for the crippled Lanc. Joe didn't have to be an aeronautical engineer to know that was a certainty. He came out of his stupor and pulling Jerry's arm, jumped from the wagon to race towards a bridge still under repair since pre-war days where they might find shelter. Just before diving to safety he was compelled to look back, drawn like Lot's wife to the conflagration behind. The bomber was on a collision course with his own house when it suddenly pulled up enough to clear the roof. He threw himself under the bridge, rolled into a knot beside Jerry and released his fear into a hellish scream while the combatting aircraft roared across the bridge violently shaking it and its occupants like an earthquake. When he caught his breath to scream again it was cut short by a torrent of tears as each boy hugged the other, joyfully aware that they were still alive and unhurt. Then all was silent. Joe moved first and cautiously gained the dyke surface to look towards his home which was still standing and showed no sign of damage. The wagon however had been reduced to splinters by gun fire as had the railing of their bridge. Jerry brought his attention around to the field where some men were stumbling out of a wrecked aircraft a hundred metres away, one of them on his knees kissing the ground. Neither one of the boys noticed the dot in the sky heading westward growing smaller and smaller.

Paddy and Joe survived the war never knowing or ever to know how their lives had for a few moments played out along the same string of fate that May morning in 1943. Paddy married his Irish sweetheart in 1944 and 11 years later emigrated to Canada followed in 1956 by his wife and four children. Joe arrived to Alberta in 1950 where he met, fell in love with and married a Dutch girl to raise their own family of four on that province's fertile farmland.

Some 70 years later the world was in the clutches of another fear. Every language in the world added the term COVID 19 to its daily use. This highly contagious novel corona virus was deadly and fearful requiring everyone to wear a face mask and avoid close contact. As the initial impact began to lose its momentum people found joy in small victories and by late Summer 2020 neighbours were once again being neighbourly.

In the little village of Wellesley Ontario, Ron and Anna, Bob and Linda had finished dinner one sunny Summer afternoon on a backyard deck when the conversation took a curious turn.

Bob to Anna: "You're Dutch, aren't you?"

Anna to Bob: "I am and I know you're Irish."

Bob: "What's your story?"

Anna: "Well, my Dad grew up in Haarlem during the war. His name was Joe."

SHOES

As soon as he noticed the shoes, Jimmy took his hand out of his pocket and walked hurriedly past the panhandler without a second glance. He was sitting legs outstretched on the pavement of the narrow bridge approaching the Lourdes grotto, forcing pedestrians to step over or go around him while he proffered an empty paper cup for alms. His collarless yellow shirt and faded jeans suggested a hard life as did the long greasy hair and untamed beard framing his too-young face.

Jimmy's approach to the holy shrine had taken him past a circus of souvenir shops and stalls selling gaudy plastic statues of saints and holy people, plastic bottles of holy water, plastic Rosary beads, hats and scarves and "genuine" relics of St. Bernadette all at 50% off today and everyday. He felt a wave of disgust and outrage that the village would approve or even allow these near-sacrilegious vendors to set up shop on one of the most holy grounds in the Christian world. As he exited this gauntlet of greed, the sight of the basilica consoled his soul and the beggar at the far end of the footbridge lifted his spirits even more. He could make better use of his money by giving to this poor unfortunate, he told himself. After all, it is a corporal work of mercy, even an obligation to give to the poor and his hand was already pulling his wallet from his pocket when he stopped. Those were not just shoes, they were signature trainers, endorsed by millionaire athletes and with a three digit price tag. How could he afford these, he wondered? It made no sense that someone in need could own these iconic shoes. Is he a drug dealer, a thief, or too lazy to work or a gang member? Too much confusion and doubt.

He quickened his pace and tried to think only of the grotto but it was useless. The shoes were a burr in his brain, a mystery needing an explanation. Abruptly he came to a full stop and looked down at his own shoes while the river of pilgrims flowed past him on either side as if he was a lifeless thing to be avoided and ignored. What did he pay for these? Seventy or seventy-five dollars? Those other shoes must have cost triple that and they looked brand new. That kind of money could buy a new shirt, new pants and some food. He turned around to look at the man but there were too many bodies to allow him to see if he was still there.

He considered going back but quickly dismissed the idea. What would he do, ask him to account for his footwear? Jimmy resumed his walk to the grotto when up ahead he saw a priest and some altar servers in procession. He had arrived just in time for Mass but all the benches were taken so he stood at the back of the congregation and joined in the celebratory prayers. As latecomers closed in around him the distraction was overwhelming and his focus evaporated. He lowered his head and started examining the nearby shoes. He saw sandals, flip-flops, bare feet, runners like his own well broken-in and looking comfortable. Some men wore loafers or leather shoes, some women had square or stiletto heels. These were ordinary footwear worn by ordinary people, none of them as costly as those at the bridge.

Somebody gave him a friendly nudge and he joined the line for Communion. He tried to funnel his thoughts into a channel of holiness to receive the Body of Christ in an elevated spiritual state, but the image of the shoes kept intruding like a schoolyard bully. His head was spinning slightly and when the priest said, "Corpus Christi," he saw the host in his right hand and a shoe in his left. "Amen" he whispered and the shoe became a ciborium releasing him momentarily from his sin as he wandered away from the crowd.

The late morning heat was unmerciful. Jimmy needed a drink of water but he wasn't going to take it from the wall of taps from which issued Lourdes Holy Water. He remembered seeing beverages in a shop window but that would mean a hike back to those horrible streets and he didn't want to cross the bridge again. An Official Bookstore near the basilica offered some hope so he entered and to his relief saw a cooler with bottled water. He paid for two and with Mass over found a bench facing the grotto with its statues of the saint and the Virgin Mary. In a few minutes he had emptied one bottle of cold, delicious water and had cracked the other one open. The water's sweetness and the absence of the din of humanity invited him to close his eyes and breathe himself slowly into a calm, settling reverie, the one he had failed to find during Mass. He sipped from the second bottle and opened his eyes hopefully to the statues, searching for what he thought he would find before he came here. Instead he noticed that Mary's feet were shrouded in a cloud and Bernadette's in a pair of simple slippers. It seemed so natural, so proper, so appropriate, so understandably the way it should be when this young peasant girl had spoken with the Mother of God. Who could ever find a quarrel or doubt the intimacy of the encounter? It was a holy moment and no one heard him say, "So be it" and no one heard him when he followed that small prayer with a sudden "Damn it all!" curse at the image of obscenely expensive runners suddenly blinding his mind's eye again. He tried to banish it, to think of anything else but the misdirection went astray and the shoes persisted.

Jimmy had enjoyed in recent years the good fortune of being able to travel and at this precise moment a particular encounter was revived chasing the shoes away. It was of another bridge, affectionately called the "Ha' penny bridge" which crossed the River Liffey in Dublin. There was a woman sitting at its entrance holding her palm out, "To feed me babby," which was wrapped in a tattered shawl across her knees. The woman looked genuinely destitute like the dirty black voluminous dress and torn cardigan she wore. She sat cross-legged displaying old broken high cut shoes tied up with string. He gave her some coins and she promised he would go straight to heaven when he died. On the heels of this another memory arrived of a man at a farmers' market dressed in a threadbare suit jacket, dark pants and cracked leather shoes that might have been brown. He handed Jimmy a piece of paper. "I'm from Chile. I have no job. My family is hungry." He looked directly into Jimmy's eyes with unadulterated sincerity. Jimmy bought him a whole chicken and a bag of bread rolls and the man simply said "Gracias" and walked away.

Other similar events paraded across Jimmy's mind; the 'teenage girl in Ottawa sitting in the middle of the sidewalk in a tourist popular arts and crafts area waving her cup and repeating over and over, "Any loose change will help please and thank you." She just stared blankly and waved her cup as couples and groups and families gave her a wide berth. Jimmy promised himself he would give her something on the way back but she was gone. He remembered being undecided in a city when the red traffic lights brought a man or woman to his car, a cardboard sign, "I haven't eaten in three days" and an empty cup shoved against his window. Were these people telling the truth or running businesses? Here on a bench in a holy place, he wondered.

He heard once on a television or a radio show a panhandler claim he could earn up to seventy thousand tax free dollars in a year by following the good weather, dressing poorly and always having an empty cup. Pocket anything you get, he had said, because people won't put money on top of money. You want them to think they haven't been given anything and you would be the first. You can give a beggar bus tickets or food vouchers if you think they would use money to buy booze or drugs, but these can be sold. Jimmy looked towards the distant bridge and thought of the shoes.

He said to himself "Scripture tells that the poor will always be with us," and he understood and he understood too that his charity would always be tested.

RETRIBUTION

St. Patrick's Day Eve, Saturday March 16 1968, 6:58 p.m. I was clanging my way up the metal staircase at the back entrance of the Daily Express heading for the Editorial Room to check the assignment board. Of all the days of the year my weekend duty rotation had to fall on this date. Arthur Guinness and I would not be sharing a barstool tonight unless the board was clear and the corner boys behaved themselves but that was wishful thinking when everyone in the world was Irish and drank green beer to prove it. Even the cops dreaded working March 17 especially when it fell on a weekend. The three local watering holes, all within two blocks of each other would be full of Celtic converts howling Danny Boy and Molly Malone until somebody lost the key and pushed another crooner out of his way to find it and that crooner bumped into one of the lads spilling his pint of black and somebody cursed at the blackguard and fisticuffs were all the rage and my friend Sgt. Gorman would hear the phone on his desk ringing and a desperate voice inviting him to the party. If charges were laid I might be able to get a few hundred words but that wouldn't happen for a few hours and I was going to be here all weekend.

At the top of the stairs I noticed a light through the partially opened door. On the other side a figure was sprawled face down across his desk, one arm dangling beside his chair, the other stretched towards a half-empty bottle of Jameson's. P.K. was asleep in his overcoat, a blank sheet of paper stuck in his typewriter and beside it a paint can and two brushes. I guessed he might have come in to work on a feature story but why tonight when he could be out celebrating his well known Irish heritage.

P.K. was a veteran reporter who had the knack of writing up the United Church Women's tea social like it was The Last Supper and all the apostles were women. When last week's heavy rains flooded a few streets he fell short of calling upon Noah to save the city from Biblical destruction. He could spin a fender bender into the tipping point of World War 111. He was the writer most responsible for the increased circulation of the newspaper since his arrival here three years ago. Letters to the editor frequently referred to something he had written. He was loved or hated to the extreme so that the publisher who was not an admirer, couldn't afford to let him go.

The scene had me puzzled. I lifted the can. It was full of green paint according to the label; exterior latex, weather resistant. But why two brushes? Someone was going to help him touch up his house, maybe. But at night? I decided to find out.

7:07 p.m. I corked the bottle out of his reach and shook his shoulders. He opened his eyes, waited for them to focus, smiled and said, "What kept ya?" I pulled a chair next to him as he straightened up momentarily then slumped back again. P.K. had put his name forward for public office once. He had his campaign photo taken at this desk, leaning forward, sleeves rolled up, a resolute expression across his face and the slogan "Give our city a fighting chance!" across the bottom. I often wondered what he was fighting for or against. He was crushed when the final tally recorded fewer than three hundred voters had put their mark next to his name.

"I gotta pee," he said, shedding his coat to the floor and shuffling his short stocky frame towards the bathroom. When he came back he looked disheveled but a bit more alert. His face and shirt were wet and he danced across the floor, his eyes twinkling with mischief and intent, his fingers clicking in rhythm with every step.

"You and I are on a mission tonight, my boy. We.........are going.......to show.....those bastards!" Emphasis falling heavily on the last word. He fetched his coat and headed for the stairs. "Bring the paint. You're driving."

What else could I do but follow if only for his own safety. 7:25 p.m. In the car he directed me east towards the outskirts of town where the city limits ended and paved road became gravel. Being unfamiliar with the area and his intentions I drove on until he told me to slow down. In the darkness I was able to make out a building just ahead.

"In here," he pointed. "Turn off the lights."

7:42 p.m. p.m. We sat in the car without saying a word for about ten minutes. It was quiet and scary. No other vehicles came along. I hoped we were going to leave sooner than later.

"Good," he said, flashing a pocket knife before my face. "To open the can. I've thought of everything. Bring the paint and brushes. Let's go."

I got out of the car still confused but more than a little curious about his plan and my part in it. He took the paint from me and set it on the cement slab outside the front door of what I decided was a small commercial building. He pried the lid off and told me to start painting the door and the railings around the step. I was still thinking about this as he slapped green paint on the window frames as high as he could reach which was never going to be to the top.

"Get to it. You're wasting our time," he hissed. "We haven't got all night."

To this day I cannot explain why I did what he told me but I did. I painted with gusto and enthusiasm, the door, the railings, the downspouts while P.K. did his best at both windows.

"That'll do. You've done a fine job. Let's get outa here."

8:11 p.m. I drove back the way we had come. P.K. was humming a tune I thought I knew. I waited until we hit the pavement then blurted out, "What the hell was that all about?"

He kept humming. I know that tune. I know that tune, I said to myself but it remained elusive. "What were we doing back there?" I demanded more forcefully hoping to draw an explanation.

"Don't worry, my boy. You'll read all about it Monday. Back to the office, I've got work to do."

I drove on and he resumed his humming.

8:40 p.m. P.K. found another mug and poured two good wallops of whisky. "Here's to a job well done," he began. "Here's to seven hundred years of servitude repaid in a small way tonight. Here's a black eye, or should I say, a green eye to imperialism. Here's to indomitable Irishry wherever green is worn. Slaintè." And he swallowed his drink in one great gulp then emptied the bottle into his cup.

"Slaintè," I whimpered while sipping my drink.

"You go home. I'm staying on a bit. I've got work to do. Go on, you've been a good sport, you have," he smiled organizing himself before his typewriter then banging away at the keys humming that tune again.

Monday March 18, 8:30 a.m. I bounded up the stairs eager to talk to P.K. about the weekend escapades and tell him I could put a name to his tune, but he wasn't coming in today, I was told. On my desk his note said I had made page three of today's issue. The editor sent me to cover a press release at city hall and he wanted the story in time for printing. That meant noon at the very latest.

2:12 p.m. I thought I would grab a paper before the three o'clock deliveries went out when I bumped into P.K. coming back from the printing bay waving a fresh copy.

"You wanted an explanation? Well here it is. Come with me. You read, I'll drive."

2:15 p.m. P.K. driving and humming. "I know that one," I started but he interrupted before I named the song. "Read page three."

I turned to page three and found his two column article. At first I could not believe what he had written especially as I was an accomplice to the act. Then I started to laugh. I laughed out loud at the contents and the sheer audacity, the brazen boldness of this little man with a big imagination and even bigger sense of daring.

His story related how, on St. Patrick's Eve leprechauns had redecorated the local Orange Lodge in Kelly Green paint. The painters must have been leprechauns, he wrote, because the wee folk were unable to reach the top of the window frames with their brushes. An anonymous phone call had alerted the Orange Order Monday morning to visit their building. After this act of devilry the leprechauns had disappeared back to Ireland.

2:34 p.m. I had finally regained control of myself as P.K. slowed the car past the Orange Lodge where half a dozen men were vigorously sanding the green paint from windows and door and railings while another stood by with a can of paint, orange, I presume. "That tune," I chuckled "The one you were humming while we were painting is called "A Nation Once Again."

"Can't you read?" he scolded. "We didn't paint anything. It was the leprechauns."

NURSES

Jen was her name, a student nurse who was trying desperately to remain calm while the razor in her hand was visibly shaking. I in my hospital bed had rolled down my pyjama bottoms to expose the area where surgery would take place the next day and Jen had poured a layer of talcum powder, north and south, east and west for the dry shave she now prepared to execute. Her nursing supervisor wasn't making it easier for either one of us. "Well? Get on with it!" She growled. Jen lowered her trembling hand. I closed my eyes and prayed.

A few weeks earlier I had removed the decaying floor boards and railings from the second storey balcony of our century home leaving the posts and beams attached to the bricks like a giant black four-legged spider. They had to come down. With rusty bolts removed, all it needed was a rope and a calculated tug from below and the structure should fall away easily enough. I wrapped the rope around my waist and used my weight against the frame until it began to sway. In no time all but one of the posts pulled away from the wall and fell onto the lawn. I tied the rope around the last post and started yanking but it wasn't moving much. Again and again I pulled until my efforts paid off but not as I expected. The doctor said I had given myself a *femoral hernia* and set a date for surgical repairs.

Ours was a small community hospital where staff and patients were very likely to pass each other in the grocery store or the wine bar. Most of the doctors lived nearby and our family physician was also an anaesthetist so I was in good and caring hands. When I checked into my semi-private room a very elderly

Mr. Fox waved feebly at me from his side of the room. He was having gastrointestinal problems and being the father of a prominent local citizen, received frequent attention from the nursing staff. Unlike Jen, these veterans were not intimidated. Mr. Fox had been helped onto his commode toilet and instructed by the nurse to get on with his business while she looked in on another patient. I heard the stream of liquid splashing on the floor and noticed Mr. Fox's passive facial expression. It seemed he was completely oblivious to the self-administered foot bath. When she returned and saw the flood below the commode she tugged the chord for room service and wagged her finger. "Mr. Fox," she scolded good-naturedly, "How many times have I told you to keep your pecker in the pot?"

Jen came in with the surgeon who briefed me on what was going to take place. She was young and gorgeous in her powder blue apron, smiling blue eyes, her whole being bubbling over with youthful enthusiasm and eagerness.

"I'm Jen," she gushed as she took my hand in hers. "I'm in my last year and I will be with you all through this procedure. It's my job to help and observe and take good care of you. This is my first surgery and I'm really looking forward to it. I'll be beside you all the time."

As she sang out these assurances she softly stroked my hand and gazed most warmly into my eyes while I was falling shamelessly in love. I wanted her to stay at my side for the rest of my life, holding my hand forever and ever more.

The surgeon interrupted my reverie. "Your G.P. will administer the anaesthetic and you have a choice. You can have a general or local anaesthetic."

Reluctantly I turned my eyes away from Jen. "What do you mean?"

"You can go under for the operation or have an epidural, like a woman has when delivering a baby. It will freeze you from your belly button to your legs and you can be awake for the surgery."

I returned my attention to the lovely Jen. I can be awake, I thought, with my hand in hers, our eyes affectionately commingling. "We'll take the local."

"Good." He said. "See you in the morning."

On his way out he passed Jen's supervisor arriving with the shaving kit. She opened it up on the table. "You'll need the towel, the powder and the razor. Shave the whole area, more than you think will be necessary. Well? Get on with it."

I swear there were chunks of broken glass and gravel spewing from her mouth as she spoke.

When she was done my angel whispered "Bye, bye," behind Attila's back leaving me alone in this suddenly dreary room with a leaky roommate for the next twelve hours. I slept fitfully, not with apprehension but with a longing for my angel of the morning, which, thank goodness, finally arrived.

An orderly brought a gurney and wheeled me out into the hall towards the operating room. Jen joined us and immediately took my hand. Oh, the rapture! Oh, the joy! She reminded me all would be well but I knew that. How else could it be with her at my side? The epidural was administered into my lower back. Attila pointed Jen to stand away from the doctors then we waited until I reported no feeling when poked with a sharp instrument. The surgeon said we could begin and deftly opened an incision.

I spent this time looking into my Jen's eyes. She seemed to be a little distressed but I was relaxed, relaxed enough to ask, "What does a hernia look like?"

A hook was inserted into the opening then drawn out with what looked like sausage skin. "Lift your head," he said. "There's the perforation."

At that moment I heard a heavy thud as if something had been dropped on the floor.

"Get her out of here!" He shouted and I watched in horror as Attila put her arms under Jen's body and dragged it through the door. The rest of the surgery has been erased from my memory. Back in my room I slept soundly for much of the day. Mr. Fox was gone when I awakened. Jen, I was told, had been sent home. Our paths never crossed again.

I was discharged from the hospital and told to take it easy for a few weeks. A VON nurse would visit me to check the stitches until my healing was complete. Three or four days later a persistent redness and sharp itching developed to the point where the nurse insisted I should have it examined by a doctor. I had an infection that was causing a build-up of fluid in the wound and it would have to be drained. At a day surgery a new incision was performed and the fluid withdrawn but it was decided to leave it open for daily flushing. A 15cm length of gauze was packed inside the opening and I went home.

The nurse arrived every afternoon to clean the opening and replace the ribbon each time with a shorter strip. One day our six-year-old son was standing at the end of the couch. He wasn't impressed as she peeled away the dressing but when she took a clasp and pulled a long pink ribbon from his Daddy's side, he was spellbound!

"That's so cool! Wow! How did you do that, Daddy?" Then he bolted out the door looking for someone to tell what he had just witnessed. After supper I explained and the new information made it even more wonderful for him. He asked if it would happen again and I told him the nurse would keep coming back until I was better. He was sitting at the porch the following afternoon when the nurse drove up. He waved and shouted hello then took off. I had scarcely stretched out on the couch and unzipped my trousers when three boys came charging into the room, my son and his two best friends.

"Watch this," he said like a magician about to perform a new trick. "It's really cool."

The nurse looked at me. I shrugged my shoulders and she got on with it telling the startled onlookers what she was doing and why. I should have asked my son if he was charging admission.

FIRE

Ten years into her marriage, Margy had learned to enjoy the simple pleasures of life; a comfortable bed, warm cozy house, flower and vegetables in her garden and the odd bottle of wine for special occasions like an anniversary or holiday. But long held fears and personal experiences were still part of her being and often determined her behaviour. This day she decided to surprise her husband on their anniversary with a bottle of wine.

Her two daughters held either side of the stroller wherein their five-month-old brother slept as they walked towards the wine shop. Margy had come here a few times before but she was alone or with Harve. She watched some customers coming out clutching their purchase, grown-ups without children and at that moment decided her husband would not be drinking wine tonight. A wine shop was not a place for children, she reasoned. They might be wrongly influenced and make bad decisions when they reached their 'teen years. She remembered a sign at the checkout about it being illegal for persons under the age of 19 years to handle alcoholic beverages. What if six-year-old Amanda grabbed a bottle with a kangaroo on the label, "How about this one, Mama?" Surveillance cameras were everywhere and Amanda would be spotted immediately. She visualized a team of helmeted, heavily armoured liquor control stormtroopers surrounding her terrified screaming child, pointing champagne bottles at her, corks ready to be unleashed. "Put the kangaroo down and step away from the bargain bin." She couldn't go through the door. Harve would have to be happy with sparkling water and an apple pie.

Margy wasn't a prude nor did she suffer from paranoia. At 38 she had become a modern woman with a cellphone, her own small car, a three bedroom bungalow on two acres equipped with modern electric appliances, electric heating and cooling systems. Natural gas was available where she lived but it was never an option. Since her honeymoon, Margy was deathly afraid of fire. Earlier this year that fear had been amplified when the church in which they were married had been damaged beyond repair by an arsonist who, authorities said, had used a bottle of whisky as an ignitor. The charred shell of the church was still cordoned off by police ribbons while insurance companies argued whether the act of a pyromaniac released them from a payout.

She had grown up in a large family, the third of five children, her God-fearing parents providing everything for their safety and well-being but leaving them on their own when it came to the nuances of life. When she and Harve began their chaste courtship, she didn't know how to act and no guidance was given by mother or father. He was her first and only romance. The first time he took her hand, she turned it into a "dead fish." The first time he tried to kiss her, she moved her head downward and his lips landed fully on her nose. The night he professed his love for her under a full moon, she said, "What are you trying to do?"

In the sixth month of their courtship Harve proposed and she stammered her acceptance without thinking. He threw his arms around her and kissed her a longer than usual kiss. She suddenly pushed him away when she felt his tongue between her lips. Harve tried to explain as best he could and to his surprise she kissed him back and followed his lead. A very pleasing physical and emotional thrill enflamed the entirety of her body and mind and when they drew apart, she said, "Yes. Yes. Let's get married."

A few days before the ceremony Margy's mother caught her completely off guard.

"There's something you need to know, umm, you should be ready to know, for, you know, your first night. Mmm it might help if you think about money."

Margy looked at her in horror and confusion.

"I mean imagine you have four coins. Picture four coins in your mind when you and Harve, mmm.....consummate your marriage."

That was a new word for Margy. She wondered if it meant 'consumer' and was even more baffled.

Her mother continued. "Think of a penny and move your, mm, hips to the left. Then think of a nickel and move them to the right."

Margy noticed her mother's body moving slightly whenever she gave directions.

This woman who had never shown any intimacy or warmth was struggling with embarrassment and determination to help her daughter as if it was her final duty before she lost her to Harve.

She swallowed and went on. "Now when you think of a dime, mmm push your hips forward and when you think of a quarter, bring them back." She did not align any movement with these words.

"Do that and all will be fine," she said, releasing her hands and rushing into the kitchen leaving Margy in stunned silence. She took a few deep breaths and headed to the bathroom locking the door behind her. In front of the mirror she put into motion what her mother had instructed. A smile of understanding illuminated her face and after two or three rhythmical sets of numbers, she leaned into the mirror and asked, "Got any loose change, Margy?"

Their honeymoon was going to be a short one, three days in a city hotel, a very unremarkable hotel at that. Later they would enjoy a proper holiday to a more exotic destination. But as events unfolded, those days became the stuff of legend, a spectacular blaze of undignified glory never to be outdone.

They arrived at their room about midnight having slipped away early from the reception everyone was enjoying. Harve wasted no time fetching his pyjamas from his baggage and finding the bathroom. Margy was holding her nighty up when he came out and hugged her. "Go on, sweetheart, I'll be waiting in the bed." She took her time changing, fixing her hair, pinching her cheeks, making herself look right. When she opened the door she gasped at the magical scene greeting her. Shaped into a heart from where she stood along the floor to the night tables were twenty lit candles turning the room into a romantic glowing invitation from Harve, the wonderful man who once again had caught her by surprise. He was reclining against propped pillows, his pyjamas thrown across a chair. Margy held out her arms. "Oh, Harve. It's so beautiful! I love it! I love you!" She turned down the covers, slipped out of her nighty and stretched out between the sheets.

When Harve's hand found her breasts, those old reservations she thought she had long lost seized her body and she went as rigid as an ironing board. Harve responded with sensitivity kissing her cheek, whispering how beautiful she was, slowly moving his body across hers. Her fearful anticipation started to dissolve as she unexpectedly remembered her mother's financial planning advice.

Penny and…..a nickel……and a dime…..and a quarter.

Penny and a nickel and a dime and a quarter.

Penny, nickel, dime, quarter,

Dime and a quarter,

Dime and quarter.

She thought she heard Harve whisper, "Fire, fire."

Dime and quarter.

"Fire!" He said louder with mounting excitement. Then he stopped moving.

"Not now!" She said. "Don't stop now! I want fire too! I want…."

"No look. The pillow is on fire! The candle! Get up quick! We have to put it out!"

He raced to the bathroom and turned on a tap while she grabbed a slipper and started pounding the candles into the floor. In seconds the pillow was in flames. Margy was jumping up and down as Harve attacked the fire with a wet towel and smoke swirled around the two of them like a mini tornado. It was then that each saw the other for the first time.

Naked.

Excited.

Wobbly bits flying hither and thither, their act of

consummation consumed by a scorched bed.

"Harve, you're a real man!"

"Oh Margy, you're so lovely all over!"

He threw the towel across the blackened pillow and moved towards his bride when a loud knocking on the door stopped him and a man's voice called,

"Are you all right? I heard screaming. Are you all right?"

Harve composed himself. "Yes. Everything's fine. We're on our honeymoon. We're O.K."

"I thought I smelled smoke."

"Not from here," said Harve assuredly.

"Well try to keep it down, sir. The hotel has other guests."

Margy put her hands across her mouth to suppress a giggle. "We could have burned the hotel down. We could have been charged with arson, spent our first night in jail." Harve wanted to laugh but stifled the urge and turned on the bathroom fan. "We'll clean up in the morning."

Next day, having hastily dressed in agreed silence, they gathered what remained of the candles into a bag and scraped the spilled wax from the floor and tables with credit cards. The burnt pillow was stuffed into Harve's pyjamas. Satisfied that they had cleaned up as well as was possible, they hugged each other and went downstairs.

The desk clerk who was a long time employee, knew how to maintain a neutral expression when dealing with guests of various temperaments and expectations. He knew that soap and towels and mini liquors were always being taken as souvenirs but later as he recounted, Harve and Margy were originals.

"You have a wonderful hotel here," Margy remarked as she turned in their card key along with a fifty dollar bill.

"That's for a pillow." Explained Harve. "We're taking one home as a memento of our honeymoon."

They were out of the door before the clerk could respond but if they had glanced back they might have noticed the spark of a smile beginning to lighten his face.

AFTERTHOUGHT

Some clear Spring night in a northern clime
when the world is still and the hour grown old
and you weary of life and your bed's just there
and dreams lie waiting to take you away,
let fall the heaviness, find resolve,
put on your coat and drive out beyond
bricks and lamps and asphalt roads
to an open rise and stand there alone
and lift your eyes to follow your breath
up to the vast and ebony vault
that draws and draws your renascent heart
into the star regaled mystery of God,
then open your soul and let Him ignite
graces as dazzling as transfigured light.

*

www.ingramcontent.com/pod-product-compliance
Lightning Source LLC
Chambersburg PA
CBHW071103040426
42443CB00013B/3387